Rolf Heimann's
AMAZING MAZES

2 TWO

Watermill Press

First published in USA by Watermill Press, an imprint of Troll Associates, Inc.

Copyright © 1994 Rolf Heimann

Printed in USA

ISBN 0-8167-3674-X
10 9 8 7 6 5 4 3 2 1

Amazing History

This maze on the right can be found on the floor of the cathedral of Chartres in France. Years ago, pilgrims who could not afford the time and money to travel to Jerusalem made their way through the maze on their knees. This was a kind of substitute trip to the Holy Land. When pilgrims could afford to go there by plane, the maze was no longer used, except by children who amused themselves during long church services! These days the maze is usually covered by rows of chairs, so that children will no longer interrupt the church services with their laughter.

Mazes are irresistible to many people, not only when they are bored. Since you are no longer able to walk your way through the Chartres maze, I have redrawn it for you here. So, pilgrim, progress through it and the rest of the book, with my best wishes for a safe and successful journey.

My name appears on every page of this book. It's "CONNY". Apart from the CONNY in this corner it appears 5 more times on this page. Solutions start on page 28.

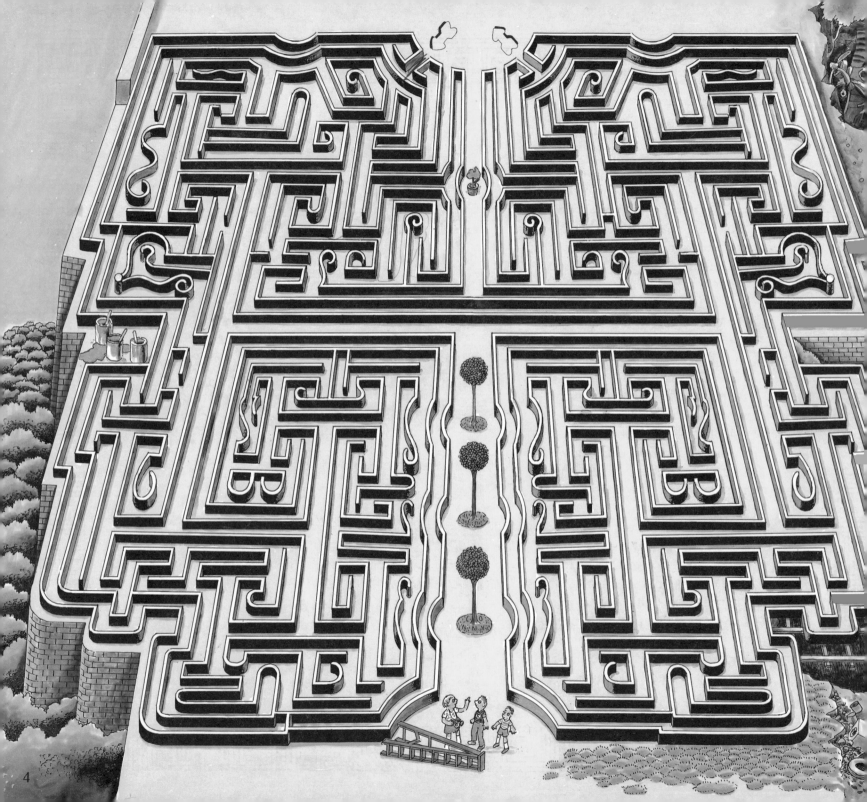

Half and half

s maze looks much too
...cult for me," said Ben.
..ybe it is," agreed Lila, "so here
...int for you: turn right 8 times.
...that you're on your own.
...you go with him. When you
...the top, it's you who has to
...the way back - but not the
...e way! You have to come back
...ugh the other half. And let me
...ou - the two halves are not
...e the same."

...at are you going to do?" Ben
...d Lila.

...going to put up that
...er and search for the three
...s that make the left half
...rent from the right half."

Ben will always take the easiest maze, Lila the hardest and Tom the one in between.

Only one of the entrances leads to the tower. Can you find it ?

2 Snail trails

There's been a disaster at the International Snail Research Ce[ntre]. Who would have believed that [the] snails would be strong enough [to] break out? There were 3 kinds: the Californian Pink Foot, the Tasmanian Wriggle-tail and the Nanasato Green. Luckily the[y] left their trails behind so that they can be traced. This is the children's job. Lila will try to collect all the Wriggle-tails, Tom the Pink Foots and Ben the Nanasato Greens.

If those snails keep escaping, I recommend snail insurance!

8

nk the ice is breaking up," Lila. "We had better get back e boat. Ben, take the shortest back, and Tom, you collect icnic basket. I'm going back e to close the door of the n hut. Someone forgot to it. I'll meet you back on hip!"

Don't you just love their suits!

This game is called one-upmanship. Find your way from top to bottom by picking things that are one-up on the next. It is possible that there is more than one way through!

For instance: this table has more legs than I...

...but us white ants can eat wooden tables...

...but I can speak better than any duck!

quack!

Solution on page 28.

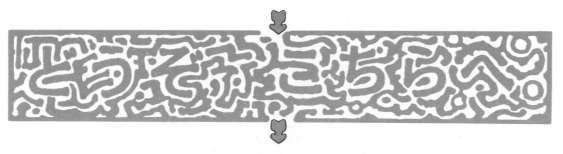

Time limit : 30 seconds.

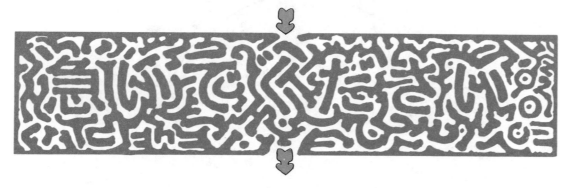

Time limit : 20 seconds.

Time limit : 30 seconds.

Time limit : 20 seconds.

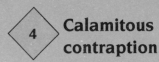

4 Calamitous contraption

Will it work? That depends not only on the specially bred Madagascan Malstock Beast, but on how well the children ca[n] operate the contraption. Ben w[ill] apply the brakes, but will he ha[ve] to pull the lever up or down? A[nd] which way does Tom turn the wheel to lower the carrot? It is Lila's job to find out whether th[e] vehicle will move backward or forward once it is in motion.

I wish they would add a propeller!

Coconut confusion

Tom and Lila went to visit friends in Samoa. Lila will guide Uncle Tufia's canoe [throu]gh the coral reefs so that [he can] deliver his fresh coconuts [to th]e ship. Tom wants to come [along], too.

["A]fraid not," said Uncle Tufia. ["My] boat is already overloaded, [but I] will give you a lift on the [way] back. Make your way to the [little h]ouse right near the ship [and] wait for us there."

[Meanw]hile Ben was fishing with [his fr]iends Elisa and Josefa. Can [you h]elp Ben work out who has [caugh]t the fish?

I hope they checked the tides...

Stepping stones

Make your way from top to bottom by following these rules:

 Scissors can cut paper

 Paper can wrap stone

 Stone can blunt scissors

 Water can extinguish fire

 Fire can burn paper

13

"I don't know why," said Tom, "this place gives me the creeps glad we're out of it."

"Bad news," laughed Lila. "You have to go back because I thin you left your cap in there!"

Tom touched his head. "You're right! And it's my favorite red one. But what about you, Lila? looks like you forgot your whit socks. And Ben, haven't you lo one of your shoes? Come on, all go back and find the way to lost property."

I'm not so sure about that. Try it anyway. I'll wait here and watch.

Wait for me! I'll have to look for my name!

If it's true that the letters "CONNY" are hidde on every page...

"I read somewhere that you'll find your way out of any maze by keeping your hand on the wall and walking until you find the exit," said Tom.
"Let's try it. I'll go along the right-hand wall and Ben, you go along the left-hand one. Let's see who'll be out first!"
"That's not fair," said Ben.
"The inside wall is shorter, so you'll be out first!"

14

15

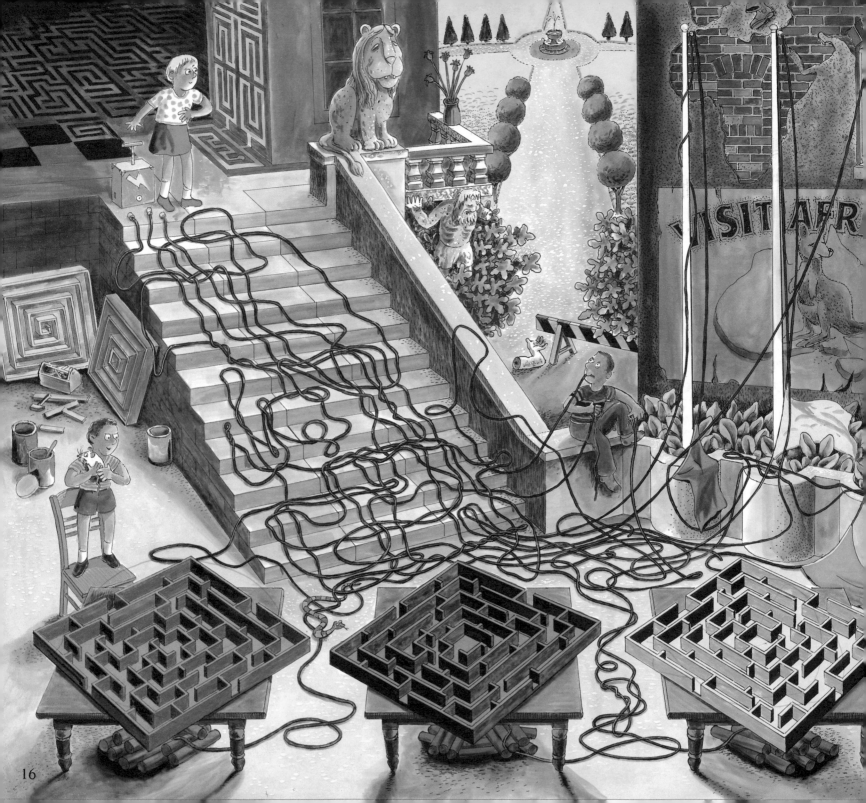

Ben's blunder

[Ben ha]s built some mazes for
[his pe]t rat, but he has made a
[mistak]e with one of them: it has
[no wa]y out at all. He has decided
[to des]troy the maze so that none
[of his p]ets are driven to madness.
[He is] ready to blow it up, and is
[waiting] for Tom to hoist the flag
[showing] the color of the faulty
[maze.] Let's hope none of them
[make] a mistake!

Don't you see it's all a mistake!

These kids have watched too much TV!

Colorful connection

Find the odd one out!
If you are having trouble,
the title of this puzzle
might give you a clue.
Or is it a red herring?

Solution on page 28.

Time limit : 30 seconds.   **Time limit : 20 seconds.**

What is it that these images have in common?

Solution on page 28.

Save the beetle !
Time limit: 20 seconds.

This waterslide into the hot springs looks like fun! Ben w to splash into the hot pool, T likes the hotter one and Lila would like to try the hottest. Now all they have to do is fin their way through the right entrance and up to the corre starting platform.

Conny is not going down those tubes!

HOT

HOTTER

HOTTEST

THE
RICHARD MILHOUSE
MEMORIAL
WATER SLIDE

Match and swirl

the look of that maze, but
: do we have to go?"
 Tom.
k we'll know when we find
atching objects," said Lila.
 go!"

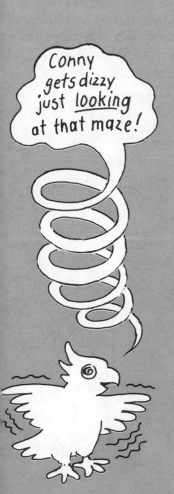

Conny gets dizzy just *looking* at that maze!

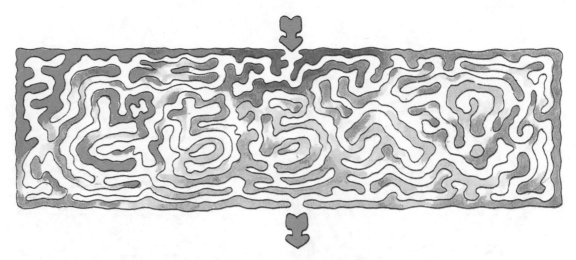

Time limit : 20 seconds.

Make your way to the center in less than 30 seconds!

21

Barrel boggle
Which barrel will fill with water?

Time limit : 20 seconds.
Good luck!

You should be able to escape
from the center in all four
directions. By the way, the picture
is not hung the right way. To help
you find north, south, east and
west, here are the Japanese
symbols for each compass point
which can be matched to the
shapes in the maze:

North   South   East   West

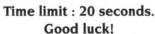
北　南　東　西

10 Chow chase

Ben, Tom and Lila want to eat
their favorite restaurant in Ba...
the famous Bamboo Palace.
However, after the bridge was
destroyed in a flood, it's not s...
easy to find the way. Lila will ...
using any path. Tom will go by
bicycle, which means that he c...
use any path except the ones
with steps. Ben has decided t...
go by taxi, and he will show th...
driver which way to go. Let's h...
there are no roadworks blocki...
the way!

Burung kakaktua hinggap di jendela

One day
I'll find
out what
they're
singing
about...

Parcelled problems

Tom and Ben have to make urgent deliveries. Because narrow lanes are so hard to get through, they find it easier to find a way over the rooftops.

Can you help them to find the best way to deliver their packages to the right owner?

Time limit : 30 seconds.

Vexing vine

Three minstrels have come to serenade the beautiful princess. Unfortunately they did not know about the fast-growing lawyer-vine. As dawn arrives they find themselves shackled by the vine tentacles. The only way to save the minstrels is to chop each plant off at the stem. Ben will save the bongo-drummer, Tom will save the alphorn player and Lila will save the lutist.

26

Solutions

One-upmanship - page: 9

The table has more legs than Conny, but white ants can eat the table, the anteater can eat the ants, a centipede has more legs than an anteater, but the snake is longer, the elephant is heavier, but the airplane can fly, the ship can carry more passengers, but the sailing ship does not need fuel, the house cannot sink, but the skyscraper has more windows, the moon is higher, but the hippopotamus has more letters in its name! The parrot, though, is more colorful, the fish can lay more eggs, but the light bulb is much brighter, but the hammer can smash the light bulb, the chest of drawers has more handles, the fire can burn the chest, but the rain can extinguish the fire. The umbrella can keep rain off, a duck doesn't need an umbrella, but a cockatoo can speak better than a duck! Try to find a different way, and don't be afraid to be silly: it's silly anyway to try to be one-up on others!

Colorful connection - page: 17

The hat is the odd one out. It is the only square that does not contain the color red.

Solution to puzzle on page 18

The images have the number 2 in common. Two eyes, two wheels, two birds, etc.

1 ▷ Half and half

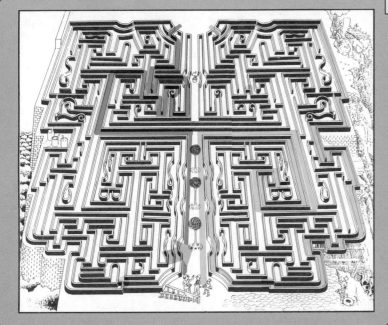

2 ▷ Snail trails

3 ⬣ Frozen footpath

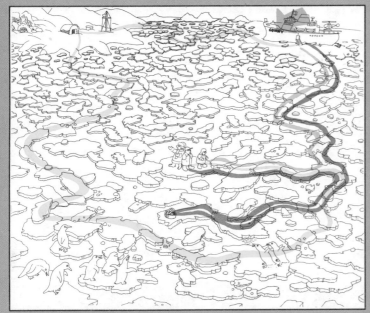

4 ▷ Calamitous contraption

Yellow - Lila   Pink - Tom   Blue - Ben

Green arrow - Conny's name

29

5 Coconut confusion

6 Lost property

7 Ben's blunder

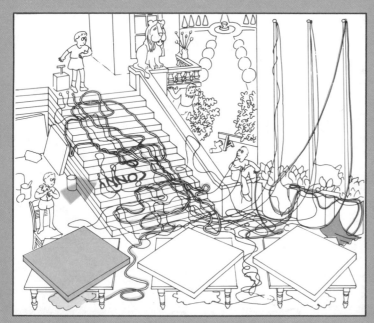

8 Tangled tubes

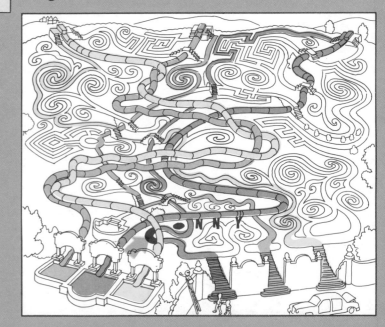

9 Match and swirl

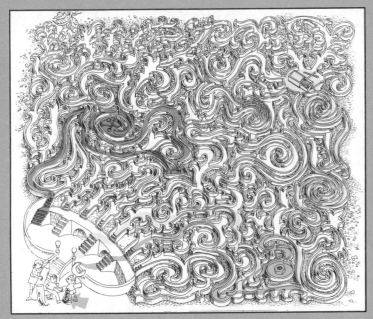

10 Chow chase

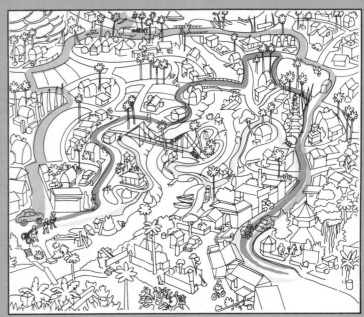

11 Parcelled problems

12 Vexing vine

"Let's do an amazing experiment," suggested Tom. "Both of us will keep our hands on the left-hand side wall and walk at the same speed until we come out again. When we meet each other, we'll call out and Lila will know we're exactly halfway through."

"Hmm, we'll see," said Lila. "Ready, set, go!"